Cato

CATO;

A Tragedy, IN FIVE ACTS,

By Joseph Addison, Esq

As Performed At The Theatre Royal,
Covent Garden.

Printed Under *the* Authority *of the* Managers
from the Prompt Book

With Remarks *by* Mrs. Inchbald

Paris, Printed *for* Baudry, English, Italian, Spanish,
Portuguese *&* German Library,
Rue Du Coq-Saint-Honoré.

Watchmaker Publishing
1823

ISBN 978-1-60386-377-3

Remarks

The author of this tragedy, to whose vigorous mind the English are indebted for their choicest moral works, came into the world with a frame so weak, that he was christened immediately on his birth, in consequence of the symptoms he gave of a speedy dissolution. The hand which reared him did a more than ordinary service to the age in which he lived, and to succeeding generations. Addison's pious writings, untainted by the rigour of superstition, have softened the harsh spirit of ancient religion, whilst they have confirmed all its principles.

He was the son of the Reverend Launcelot Addison, Rector of Milston, in the county of Wilts, at which place he was born, on the 6th of May, 1672.

After passing through some inferior schools, he was placed at the Charter-House; where he contracted that intimacy with Steele, which grew to a friendship honourable to them both, from its duration, and the instructions which their joint labour bestowed on mankind.

At the age of fifteen, young Addison was entered at Queen's College, Oxford, where he applied himself so closely to study, that, in a few years, his Latin poetry gained him high reputation in both universities, and, at the age of twenty-two, he became known to the nation at large by his English compositions.

He was now pressed by his father to take holy orders; which, notwithstanding his sedate turn of mind, and his habits of piety, he positively refused. Mr. Tickell has alleged, that it was Addison's extreme modesty, a constitutional timidity, which made him resolve against being in the church–but he became a statesman; and, surely, that is a character which requires as much courage as a clergyman's, when the church is not under persecution.

The first dramatic work from the pen of Addison, was an opera called "Rosamond," which having but indifferent success, he next assisted Steele in his play of "The Tender Husband;" for which the author surprised him by a dedication, openly to avow the obligation.

These two friends now united their efforts in that well-known periodical work, "The Spectator;" by which they reformed the manners, as well as the morals, of their readers, and established their own literary fame. But, as the talents of Addison were superior to those of Steele, so are the papers in this work which were written by him esteemed above the rest;–and, as a mark of distinction, he had the laudable, or his friend Steele the honest pride, to affix a letter at the end of every such paper, by which it should be known for his. The Muse Clio furnished the four letters which have been thus used in "The Spectator," as Addison's honourable stamp of authorship.

In the periodical work of "The Guardian" he had likewise some share; and, in 1713, he produced, what Dr. Johnson has called "the noblest work of Addison's genius"–"Cato."

Notwithstanding the merit of this play, it is certain that it was indebted to the political circumstances of the times, for that enthusiastic applause with which it was received by the town.

The joy or sorrow which an author is certain to experience upon every new production, is far more powerful in the heart of a dramatist than in that of any other writer. The sound of clamorous plaudits raises his spirits to a kind of ecstasy; whilst hisses and groans, from a dissatisfied audience, strike on the ear like a personal insult, avowing loud and public contempt for that in which he has been labouring to show his skill.

Addison, with his timid nature, felt all the excruciating tortures of an ambitious, yet a fearful dramatist. He could not stay at home on the first night of "Cato;" for to be told, at once, that his tragedy was driven from the stage with derision, had been to his tremulous nerves like the dart of death. Not less peril might have befallen him as an auditor–he therefore was neither present on the first performance, nor absent from the theatre;–but, placing himself on a bench in the green-room, his body motionless, his soul in tumult, he kept by his side a friend, whom he dispatched every minute towards the stage, to bring him news of what was passing there. He thus secured, he conceived, progressive information of his fate, without the risk of hearing it from an enraged multitude. But such was the vehemence of applause, that shouts of admiration forced their way through the walls of the green-room, before his messenger could return with the gladsome tidings. Yet, not till the last sentence was spoken, and the curtain fairly dropped upon Cato and his weeping friends, did the author venture to move from the inanimate position in which he was fixed. This acute dread of failure now heightened the joy of success, and never was success more complete.

"Cato," says Pope, in a letter to one of his friends, written at the time, "was not so much the wonder of Rome in his days, as he is of Britain in ours."

The most fortunate of all occurrences took place, from the skill with which Addison drew this illustrious Roman—he gave him so much virtue, that both Whigs and Tories declared him of their party; and instead of any one, on either side, opposing his sentences in the cause of freedom, all strove which should the most honour him.

Both auditors and readers, since that noted period, much as they may praise this tragedy, complain that it wants the very first requisite of a dramatic work—

power to affect the passions. This criticism shows, to the full extent, how men were impassioned, at that time, by their political sentiments. They brought their passions with them to the playhouse, fired on the subject of the play; and all the poet had to do was to extend the flame.

It is a charge against this drama, that the love scenes are all insipid; but it should be considered, that neither Cato nor his family, with strict propriety, could love anything but their country.—As this is a love which women feel in a much less degree than men, and as bondage, not liberty, is woman's wish, "Cato," with all his patriotism, must ever be a dull entertainment to the female sex; and men of course receive but little pleasure from elegant amusements, of which women do not partake.

The language and sentiments contained here are worthy of the great Addison and the great Cato; and if, as it is objected, the characters are too elevated to be natural, yet they accord with that idea of nature which imagination conceives of such remarkable personages.

The author of "Cato" had planned other tragedies and celebrated works, which the subsequent part of his days did not give him leisure to execute; for, on the death of Queen Anne, the Lords Justices made him their Secretary: he was soon after appointed principal Secretary of State. These, and other public employments, prevented his completing farther literary designs. Or, it may be thought, that the loss of his domestic tranquillity, at this time, by his marriage with the Countess Dowager of Warwick, might possibly impede every future attempt for the favour of the Muses, to whom this, his wife, had not the slightest affinity. It is supposed she embittered, by arrogance and discontent, the remainder of this good man's life, which terminated on the 17th of June, 1719, in the 47th year of his age. He died at Holland House, near Kensington, and left an only child, a daughter, by the Countess.

Lady Warwick had also a son by her former husband, a very fine, spirited, and accomplished youth, for whose welfare the dying Addison showed peculiar concern; for, in the extremity of his disorder, having dismissed his physicians, and with them all hopes of recovery, he desired that the young Lord Warwick might be called to his bedside. He came–but life was now fast departing from his revered father-in-law, and he uttered not a word. After an afflicting pause, the young man said, "Dear sir, you sent for me; I believe, and I hope, that you have some commands; I shall hold them most sacred." Grasping his hand, Addison softly replied, "I sent for you, that you might see in what peace a Christian can die." He spoke with difficulty, and instantly expired.

It is to this circumstance Mr. Tickell refers in his lines on Addison's death, where he has this passage:

> "He taught us how to live; and, oh! too high
> A price for knowledge, taught us how to die."

Dramatis Personæ

Cato,	Mr. Cooke.
Portius,	Mr. Siddons.
Marcus,	Mr. H. Johnston.
Sempronius,	Mr. Cory.
Juba,	Mr. Brunton.
Syphax,	Mr. Murray.
Lucius,	Mr. Claremont.
Decius,	Mr. Williams.
Lucia,	Miss Marriott.
Marcia,	Mrs. Litchfield.

Mutineers, Guards, etc.

SCENE–The Governor's Palace in Utica

Cato

Act *the* First

SCENE I

A Hall

Enter PORTIUS *and* MARCUS

Por. The dawn is overcast, the morning low'rs, And heavily in clouds brings on the day, The great, the important day, big with the fate Of Cato and of Rome—Our father's death Would fill up all the guilt of civil war, And close the scene of blood. Already Cæsar Has ravaged more than half the globe, and sees Mankind grown thin by his destructive sword: Should he go farther, numbers would be wanting To form new battles, and support his crimes. Ye gods, what havoc does ambition make Among your works!

Marc. Thy steady temper, Portius, Can look on guilt, rebellion, fraud, and Cæsar, In the calm lights of mild philosophy; I'm tortured e'en to madness, when I think On the proud victor–ev'ry time he's named, Pharsalia rises to my view!–I see Th'

insulting tyrant, prancing o'er the field, Strew'd with
Rome's citizens, and drench'd in slaughter; His
horse's hoofs wet with patrician blood! Oh, Portius!
is there not some chosen curse, Some hidden
thunder in the stores of Heav'n, Red with
uncommon wrath, to blast the man Who owes his
greatness to his country's ruin?

Por. Believe me, Marcus, 'tis an impious greatness,
And mix'd with too much horror to be envied: How
does the lustre of our father's actions, Through the
dark cloud of ills that cover him, Break out, and
burn with more triumphant brightness! His
sufferings shine, and spread a glory round him;
Greatly unfortunate, he fights the cause Of honour,
virtue, liberty, and Rome. His sword ne'er fell, but
on the guilty head; Oppression, tyranny, and pow'r
usurp'd, Draw all the vengeance of his arm upon
them.

Marc. Who knows not this? but what can Cato do
Against a world, a base, degenerate world, That
courts the yoke, and bows the neck to Cæsar? Pent
up in Utica, he vainly forms A poor epitome of
Roman greatness, And, cover'd with Numidian
guards, directs A feeble army, and an empty senate,
Remnants of mighty battles fought in vain. By
Heav'n, such virtue, join'd with such success,
Distracts my very soul! Our father's fortune Would
almost tempt us to renounce his precepts.

Por. Remember what our father oft has told us: The
ways of Heav'n are dark and intricate, Puzzled in

mazes, and perplex'd with errors; Our understanding traces them in vain, Lost and bewilder'd in the fruitless search; Nor sees with how much art the windings run, Nor where the regular confusion ends.

Marc. These are suggestions of a mind at ease:– Oh, Portius! didst thou taste but half the griefs That wring my soul, thou couldst not talk thus coldly. Passion unpitied, and successless love, Plant daggers in my heart, and aggravate My other griefs.–Were but my Lucia kind——

Por. Thou see'st not that thy brother is thy rival; But I must hide it, for I know thy temper.   [*Aside.* Behold young Juba, the Numidian prince, With how much care he forms himself to glory, And breaks the fierceness of his native temper, To copy out our father's bright example. He loves our sister Marcia, greatly loves her; His eyes, his looks, his actions, all betray it; But still the smother'd fondness burns within him; When most it swells, and labours for a vent, The sense of honour, and desire of fame, Drive the big passion back into his heart. What! shall an African, shall Juba's heir, Reproach great Cato's son, and show the world A virtue wanting in a Roman soul?

Marc. Portius, no more! your words leave stings behind them. Whene'er did Juba, or did Portius, show A virtue that has cast me at a distance, And thrown me out in the pursuits of honour?

Por. Marcus, I know thy gen'rous temper well; Fling but the appearance of dishonour on it, It straight takes fire, and mounts into a blaze.

Marc. A brother's suff'rings claim a brother's pity.

Por. Heav'n knows, I pity thee—Behold my eyes, Ev'n whilst I speak–Do they not swim in tears? Were but my heart as naked to thy view, Marcus would see it bleed in his behalf.

Marc. Why then dost treat me with rebukes, instead Of kind condoling cares, and friendly sorrow?

Por. Oh, Marcus! did I know the way to ease Thy troubled heart, and mitigate thy pains, Marcus, believe me, I could die to do it.

Marc. Thou best of brothers, and thou best of friends! Pardon a weak distemper'd soul, that swells With sudden gusts, and sinks as soon in calms, The sport of passions. But Sempronius comes: He must not find this softness hanging on me.

[*Exit* MARCUS

Enter SEMPRONIUS

Sem. Conspiracies no sooner should be form'd Than executed. What means Portius here? I like not that cold youth. I must dissemble, And speak a language foreign to my heart.   [*Aside*

Good-morrow, Portius; let us once embrace, Once more embrace, while yet we both are free. To-morrow, should we thus express our friendship, Each might receive a slave into his arms; This sun, perhaps, this morning sun's the last That e'er shall rise on Roman liberty.

Por. My father has this morning call'd together To this poor hall, his little Roman senate, (The leavings of Pharsalia) to consult If he can yet oppose the mighty torrent That bears down Rome and all her gods before it, Or must at length give up the world to Cæsar.

Sem. Not all the pomp and majesty of Rome Can raise her senate more than Cato's presence. His virtues render our assembly awful, They strike with something like religious fear, And make even Cæsar tremble at the head Of armies flush'd with conquest. Oh, my Portius! Could I but call that wond'rous man my father, Would but thy sister Marcia be propitious To thy friend's vows, I might be blest indeed!

Por. Alas, Sempronius! wouldst thou talk of love To Marcia, whilst her father's life's in danger? Thou might'st as well court the pale, trembling vestal, When she beholds the holy flame expiring.

Sem. The more I see the wonders of thy race, The more I'm charm'd. Thou must take heed, my Portius; The world has all its eyes on Cato's son; Thy father's merit sets thee up to view, And shows thee in the fairest point of light, To make thy virtues or thy faults conspicuous.

Por. Well dost thou seem to check my ling'ring here In this important hour–I'll straight away, And while the fathers of the senate meet In close debate, to weigh th' events of war, I'll animate the soldiers' drooping courage With love of freedom and contempt of life; I'll thunder in their ears their country's cause, And try to rouse up all that's Roman in them. 'Tis not in mortals to command success, But we'll do more, Sempronius–we'll deserve it.   [*Exit*

Sem. Curse on the stripling! how he apes his sire! Ambitiously sententious–But I wonder Old Syphax comes not; his Numidian genius Is well disposed to mischief, were he prompt And eager on it; but he must be spurr'd, And every moment quicken'd to the course. Cato has used me ill; he has refused His daughter Marcia to my ardent vows. Besides, his baffled arms, and ruin'd cause, Are bars to my ambition. Cæsar's favour, That show'rs down greatness on his friends, will raise me To Rome's first honours. If I give up Cato, I claim, in my reward, his captive daughter. But Syphax comes—

Enter SYPHAX

Syph. Sempronius, all is ready; I've sounded my Numidians, man by man, And find them ripe for a revolt: they all Complain aloud of Cato's discipline, And wait but the command to change their master.

Sem. Believe me, Syphax, there's no time to waste; Ev'n while we speak, our conqueror comes on, And gathers ground upon us every moment. Alas! thou know'st not Cæsar's active soul, With what a dreadful course he rushes on From war to war. In vain has nature form'd Mountains and oceans t'oppose his passage; He bounds o'er all. One day more Will set the victor thund'ring at our gates. But, tell me, hast thou yet drawn o'er young Juba? That still would recommend thee more to Cæsar, And challenge better terms.

Syph. Alas! he's lost! He's lost, Sempronius; all his thoughts are full Of Cato's virtues–But I'll try once more (For every instant I expect him here) If yet I can subdue those stubborn principles Of faith and honour, and I know not what, That have corrupted his Numidian temper, And struck th' infection into all his soul.

Sem. Be sure to press upon him every motive. Juba's surrender, since his father's death, Would give up Afric into Cæsar's hands, And make him lord of half the burning zone.

Syph. But is it true, Sempronius, that your senate Is call'd together? Gods! thou must be cautious; Cato has piercing eyes, and will discern Our frauds, unless they're cover'd thick with art.

Sem. Let me alone, good Syphax, I'll conceal My thoughts in passion ('tis the surest way); I'll bellow out for Rome, and for my country, And mouth at

Cæsar, till I shake the senate. Your cold hypocrisy's a stale device, A worn-out trick: wouldst thou be thought in earnest, Clothe thy feign'd zeal in rage, in fire, in fury!

Syph. In troth, thou'rt able to instruct grey hairs, And teach the wily African deceit.

Sem. Once more be sure to try thy skill on Juba. Remember, Syphax, we must work in haste; Oh, think what anxious moments pass between The birth of plots, and their last fatal periods! Oh, 'tis a dreadful interval of time, Fill'd up with horror all, and big with death! Destruction hangs on every word we speak, On every thought, till the concluding stroke Determines all, and closes our design.   [*Exit.*

Syph. I'll try if yet I can reduce to reason This headstrong youth, and make him spurn at Cato. The time is short; Cæsar comes rushing on us– But hold! young Juba sees me, and approaches!

Enter JUBA

Jub. Syphax, I joy to meet thee thus alone. I have observed of late thy looks are fall'n, O'ercast with gloomy cares and discontent; Then tell me, Syphax, I conjure thee, tell me, What are the thoughts that knit thy brow in frowns, And turn thine eye thus coldly on thy prince?

Syph. 'Tis not my talent to conceal my thoughts, Or carry smiles and sunshine in my face, When discontent sits heavy at my heart; I have not yet so much the Roman in me.

Jub. Why dost thou cast out such ungenerous terms Against the lords and sov'reigns of the world? Dost thou not see mankind fall down before them, And own the force of their superior virtue? Is there a nation in the wilds of Afric, Amidst our barren rocks and burning sands, That does not tremble at the Roman name?

Syph. Gods! where's the worth that sets these people up Above your own Numidia's tawny sons? Do they with tougher sinews bend the bow? Or flies the javelin swifter to its mark, Launch'd from the vigour of a Roman arm? Who like our active African instructs The fiery steed, and trains him to his hand? Or guides in troops th' embattled elephant Laden with war? These, these are arts, my prince, In which your Zama does not stoop to Rome.

Jub. These all are virtues of a meaner rank: Perfections that are placed in bones and nerves. A Roman soul is bent on higher views; Turn up thy eyes to Cato; There may'st thou see to what a godlike height The Roman virtues lift up mortal man. While good, and just, and anxious for his friends, He's still severely bent against himself; And when his fortune sets before him all The pomps and pleasures that his soul can wish, His rigid virtue will accept of none.

Syph. Believe me, prince, there's not an African That traverses our vast Numidian deserts In quest of prey, and lives upon his bow, But better practises those boasted virtues. Coarse are his meals, the fortune of the chase; Amidst the running stream he slakes his thirst; Toils all the day, and, at the approach of night, On the first friendly bank he throws him down, Or rests his head upon a rock till morn; Then rises fresh, pursues his wonted game, And if the following day he chance to find A new repast, or an untasted spring, Blesses his stars, and thinks it luxury.

Jub. Thy prejudices, Syphax, won't discern What virtues grow from ignorance and choice, Nor how the hero differs from the brute. Where shall we find the man that bears affliction, Great and majestic in his griefs, like Cato? How does he rise against a load of woes, And thank the gods that threw the weight upon him!

Syph. 'Tis pride, rank pride, and haughtiness of soul; I think the Romans call it stoicism. Had not your royal father thought so highly Of Roman virtue, and of Cato's cause, He had not fall'n by a slave's hand inglorious.

Jub. Why dost thou call my sorrows up afresh? My father's name brings tears into my eyes.

Syph. Oh, that you'd profit by your father's ills!

Jub. What wouldst thou have me do?

Syph. Abandon Cato.

Jub. Syphax, I should be more than twice an orphan
By such a loss.

Syph. Ay, there's the tie that binds you! You long to
call him father. Marcia's charms Work in your heart
unseen, and plead for Cato. No wonder you are deaf
to all I say.

Jub. Syphax, your zeal becomes importunate; I've
hitherto permitted it to rave, And talk at large; but
learn to keep it in, Lest it should take more freedom
than I'll give it.

Syph. Sir, your great father never used me thus. Alas,
he's dead! but can you e'er forget The tender
sorrows, And repeated blessings, Which you drew
from him in your last farewell? The good old king,
at parting, wrung my hand, (His eyes brimful of
tears) then sighing cried, Pr'ythee be careful of my
son!—His grief Swell'd up so high, he could not
utter more.

Jub. Alas! thy story melts away my soul! That best of
fathers! how shall I discharge The gratitude and duty
that I owe him?

Syph. By laying up his counsels in your heart.

Jub. His counsels bade me yield to thy direction:
Then, Syphax, chide me in severest terms, Vent all
thy passion, and I'll stand its shock, Calm and

unruffled as a summer sea, When not a breath of wind flies o'er its surface.

Syph. Alas! my prince, I'd guide you to your safety.

Jub. I do believe thou wouldst; but tell me how?

Syph. Fly from the fate that follows Cæsar's foes.

Jub. My father scorn'd to do it.

Syph. And therefore died.

Jub. Better to die ten thousand thousand deaths, Than wound my honour.

Syph. Rather say, your love.

Jub. Syphax, I've promised to preserve my temper; Why wilt thou urge me to confess a flame I long have stifled, and would fain conceal?

Syph. Believe me, prince, though hard to conquer love, 'Tis easy to divert and break its force. Absence might cure it, or a second mistress Light up another flame, and put out this. The glowing dames of Zama's royal court Have faces flush'd with more exalted charms; Were you with these, my prince, you'd soon forget The pale, unripen'd beauties of the north.

Jub. 'Tis not a set of features, or complexion, The tincture of a skin, that I admire: Beauty soon grows familiar to the lover, Fades in his eye, and palls upon the sense. The virtuous Marcia tow'rs above her sex: True, she is fair (Oh, how divinely fair!), But still the lovely maid improves her charms, With inward greatness, unaffected wisdom, And sanctity of manners; Cato's soul Shines out in everything she acts or speaks, While winning mildness and attractive smiles Dwell in her looks, and, with becoming grace, Soften the rigour of her father's virtue.

Syph. How does your tongue grow wanton in her praise! But on my knees, I beg you would consider–

Jub. Ha! Syphax, is't not she?–She moves this way; And with her Lucia, Lucius's fair daughter. My heart beats thick–I pr'ythee, Syphax, leave me.

Syph. Ten thousand curses fasten on them both! Now will the woman, with a single glance, Undo what I've been lab'ring all this while.

[*Exit* SYPHAX

Enter MARCIA *and* LUCIA.

Jub. Hail, charming maid! How does thy beauty smooth The face of war, and make even horror smile! At sight of thee my heart shakes off its sorrows; I feel a dawn of joy break in upon me, And for a while forget th' approach of Cæsar.

Marcia. I should be grieved, young prince, to think my presence Unbent your thoughts, and slacken'd them to arms, While, warm with slaughter, our victorious foe Threatens aloud, and calls you to the field.

Jub. Oh, Marcia, let me hope thy kind concerns And gentle wishes follow me to battle! The thought will give new vigour to my arm, And strength and weight to my descending sword, And drive it in a tempest on the foe.

Marcia. My pray'rs and wishes always shall attend The friends of Rome, the glorious cause of virtue, And men approved of by the gods and Cato.

Jub. That Juba may deserve thy pious cares, I'll gaze for ever on thy godlike father, Transplanting one by one, into my life, His bright perfections, till I shine like him.

Marcia. My father never, at a time like this, Would lay out his great soul in words, and waste Such precious moments.

Jub. Thy reproofs are just, Thou virtuous maid; I'll hasten to my troops, And fire their languid souls with Cato's virtue. If e'er I lead them to the field, when all The war shall stand ranged in its just array, And dreadful pomp, then will I think on thee; Oh, lovely maid! then will I think on thee; And, in the shock of charging hosts, remember What glorious deeds should grace the man who hopes For Marcia's love.   [*Exit* JUBA.

Lucia. Marcia, you're too severe; How could you chide the young good-natured prince, And drive him from you with so stern an air, A prince that loves, and dotes on you to death?

Marcia. 'Tis therefore, Lucia, that I chide him from me; His air, his voice, his looks, and honest soul, Speak all so movingly in his behalf, I dare not trust myself to hear him talk.

Lucia. Why will you fight against so sweet a passion, And steel your heart to such a world of charms?

Marcia. How, Lucia! wouldst thou have me sink away In pleasing dreams, and lose myself in love, When ev'ry moment Cato's life's at stake? Cæsar comes arm'd with terror and revenge, And aims his thunder at my father's head. Should not the sad occasion swallow up My other cares?

Lucia. Why have I not this constancy of mind, Who have so many griefs to try its force? Sure, Nature form'd me of her softest mould, Enfeebled all my soul with tender passions, And sunk me ev'n below my own weak sex: Pity and love, by turns, oppress my heart.

Marcia. Lucia, disburden all thy cares on me, And let me share thy most retired distress. Tell me, who raises up this conflict in thee?

Lucia. I need not blush to name them, when I tell thee They're Marcia's brothers, and the sons of Cato.

Marcia. They both behold thee with their sister's eyes, And often have reveal'd their passion to me. But tell me, which of them is Lucia's choice?

Lucia. Suppose 'twere Portius, could you blame my choice?– Oh, Portius, thou hast stolen away my soul! Marcus is over warm, his fond complaints Have so much earnestness and passion in them, I hear him with a secret kind of horror, And tremble at his vehemence of temper.

Marcia. Alas, poor youth! How will thy coldness raise Tempests and storms in his afflicted bosom! I dread the consequence.

Lucia. You seem to plead Against your brother Portius.

Marcia. Heav'n forbid. Had Portius been the unsuccessful lover, The same compassion would have fall'n on him.

Lucia. Was ever virgin love distress'd like mine! Portius himself oft falls in tears before me As if he mourn'd his rival's ill success; Then bids me hide the motions of my heart, Nor show which way it turns– so much he fears The sad effect that it will have on Marcus.

Marcia. Let us not, Lucia, aggravate our sorrows, But to the gods submit the event of things. Our lives, discolour'd with our present woes, May still grow bright, and smile with happier hours. So the pure limpid stream, when foul with stains Of rushing torrents and descending rains, Works itself clear, and, as it runs, refines, Till, by degrees, the floating mirror shines; Reflects each flower that on the border grows, And a new heav'n in its fair bosom shows.   [*Exeunt*

Act *the* Second

Scene I

The Senate sitting

Flourish

Enter CATO

Cato. Fathers, we once again are met in council; Cæsar's approach has summon'd us together, And Rome attends her fate from our resolves. How shall we treat this bold aspiring man? Success still follows him, and backs his crimes; Pharsalia gave him Rome, Egypt has since Received his yoke, and the whole Nile is Cæsar's. Why should I mention Juba's overthrow, And Scipio's death? Numidia's burning sands Still smoke with blood. 'Tis time we should decree What course to take. Our foe advances on us, And envies us even Lybia's sultry deserts. Fathers, pronounce your thoughts: are they still fix'd To hold it out, and fight it to the last? Or are your hearts subdued at length, and wrought, By time and ill success, to a submission? Sempronius, speak.

Sem. Gods! can a Roman senate long debate Which of the two to chuse, slav'ry or death! No; let us rise at once, gird on our swords, And, at the head of our remaining troops, Attack the foe, break through the thick array Of his throng'd legions, and charge home upon him. Perhaps some arm, more lucky than the rest, May reach his heart, and free the world from bondage. Rise, fathers, rise! 'tis Rome demands your help; Rise, and revenge her slaughter'd citizens, Or share their fate!– To battle! Great Pompey's shade complains that we are slow; And Scipio's ghost walks unrevenged amongst us.

Cato. Let not a torrent of impetuous zeal Transport thee thus beyond the bounds of reason; True fortitude is seen in great exploits, That justice warrants, and that wisdom guides; All else is tow'ring phrensy and distraction. Lucius, we next would know what's your opinion.

Luc. My thoughts, I must confess, are turn'd on peace. Already have our quarrels fill'd the world With widows, and with orphans: Scythia mourns Our guilty wars, and earth's remotest regions Lie half unpeopled by the feuds of Rome: 'Tis time to sheathe the sword, and spare mankind. Already have we shown our love to Rome, Now let us show submission to the gods. We took up arms, not to revenge ourselves, But free the commonwealth; when this end fails, Arms have no further use. Our country's cause, That drew our swords, now wrests them from our hands. And bids us not delight in Roman blood, Unprofitably shed. What men could do, Is done already: Heav'n and earth will witness, If Rome must fall, that we are innocent.

Cato. Let us appear nor rash nor diffident; Immod'rate valour swells into a fault; And fear, admitted into public councils, Betrays like treason. Let us shun them both. Fathers, I cannot see that our affairs Are grown thus desp'rate: we have bulwarks round us; Within our walls are troops inured to toil In Afric's heat, and season'd to the sun; Numidia's spacious kingdom lies behind us, Ready to rise at its young prince's call. While there is hope, do not distrust the gods; But wait, at least, till Cæsar's near approach Force us to yield. 'Twill never be too late To sue for chains, and own a conqueror. Why should Rome fall a moment ere her time? No, let us draw her term of freedom out In its full length, and spin it to the last, So shall we gain still one day's liberty; And let me perish, but in Cato's judgment, A day, an hour, of virtuous liberty, Is worth a whole eternity in bondage.

Enter MARCUS.

Marc. Fathers, this moment, as I watch'd the gate, Lodged on my post, a herald is arrived From Cæsar's camp, and with him comes old Decius, The Roman knight; he carries in his looks Impatience, and demands to speak with Cato.

Cato. By your permission, fathers–bid him enter.
                                        [*Exit* MARCUS.
Decius was once my friend, but other prospects Have loosed those ties, and bound him fast to Cæsar. His message may determine our resolves.

Enter DECIUS

Dec. Cæsar sends health to Cato—

Cato. Could he send it To Cato's slaughter'd friends, it would be welcome. Are not your orders to address the senate?

Dec. My business is with Cato. Cæsar sees The straits to which you're driven; and, as he knows Cato's high worth, is anxious for your life.

Cato. My life is grafted on the fate of Rome. Would he save Cato, bid him spare his country. Tell your dictator this; and tell him, Cato Disdains a life which he has power to offer.

Dec. Rome and her senators submit to Cæsar; Her gen'rals and her consuls are no more, Who check'd his conquests, and denied his triumphs. Why will not Cato be this Cæsar's friend?

Cato. These very reasons thou hast urged forbid it.

Dec. Cato, I've orders to expostulate And reason with you, as from friend to friend: Think on the storm that gathers o'er your head, And threatens ev'ry hour to burst upon it; Still may you stand high in your country's honours— Do but comply, and make your peace with Cæsar; Rome will rejoice, and cast its eyes on Cato, As on the second of mankind.

Cato. No more; I must not think of life on such conditions.

Dec. Cæsar is well acquainted with your virtues, And therefore sets this value on your life. Let him but know the price of Cato's friendship, And name your terms.

Cato. Bid him disband his legions, Restore the commonwealth to liberty, Submit his actions to the public censure, And stand the judgment of a Roman senate. Bid him do this, and Cato is his friend.

Dec. Cato, the world talks loudly of your wisdom—

Cato. Nay, more, though Cato's voice was ne'er employ'd To clear the guilty, and to varnish crimes, Myself will mount the rostrum in his favour, And strive to gain his pardon from the people.

Dec. A style like this becomes a conqueror.

Cato. Decius, a style like this becomes a Roman.

Dec. What is a Roman, that is Cæsar's foe?

Cato. Greater than Cæsar: he's a friend to virtue.

Dec. Consider, Cato, you're in Utica, And at the head of your own little senate: You do not thunder in the capitol, With all the mouths of Rome to second you.

Cato. Let him consider that, who drives us hither. 'Tis Cæsar's sword has made Rome's senate little, And thinn'd its ranks. Alas! thy dazzled eye Beholds this man in a false glaring light, Which conquest and success have thrown upon him; Did'st thou but view him right, thou'dst see him black With murder, treason, sacrilege, and crimes That strike my soul with horror but to name them. I know thou look'st on me as on a wretch Beset with ills, and cover'd with misfortunes; But, by the gods I swear, millions of worlds Should never buy me to be like that Cæsar.

Dec. Does Cato send this answer back to Cæsar, For all his gen'rous cares and proffer'd friendship?

Cato. His cares for me are insolent and vain: Presumptuous man! the gods take care of Cato. Would Cæsar show the greatness of his soul, Bid him employ his care for these my friends, And make good use of his ill-gotten pow'r, By sheltering men much better than himself.

Dec. Your high, unconquer'd heart makes you forget You are a man. You rush on your destruction. But I have done. When I relate hereafter The tale of this unhappy embassy, All Rome will be in tears.

[*Exit* DECIUS

Sem. Cato, we thank thee. The mighty genius of immortal Rome Speaks in thy voice; thy soul breathes liberty. Cæsar will shrink to hear the words thou utter'st, And shudder in the midst of all his conquests.

Luc. The senate owns its gratitude to Cato, Who with so great a soul consults its safety, And guards our lives, while he neglects his own.

Sem. Sempronius gives no thanks on this account. Lucius seems fond of life; but what is life? 'Tis not to stalk about, and draw fresh air From time to time, or gaze upon the sun; 'Tis to be free. When liberty is gone, Life grows insipid.

Cato. Come; no more, Sempronius; All here are friends to Rome, and to each other. Let us not weaken still the weaker side By our divisions.

Sem. Cato, my resentments Are sacrificed to Rome–I stand reproved.

Cato. Fathers, 'tis time you come to a resolve.

Luc. Cato, we all go in to your opinion; Cæsar's behaviour has convinced the senate We ought to hold it out till terms arrive.

Sem. We ought to hold it out till death; but, Cato, My private voice is drown'd amidst the senate's.

Cato. Then let us rise, my friends, and strive to fill This little interval, this pause of life (While yet our liberty and fates are doubtful) With resolution, friendship, Roman bravery, And all the virtues we can crowd into it; That Heav'n may say, it ought to be prolong'd. Fathers, farewell–The young Numidian prince Comes forward, and expects to know our counsels.   [*Exeunt* SENATORS

Enter JUBA

Juba, the Roman senate has resolved, Till time give better prospects, still to keep The sword unsheathed, and turn its edge on Cæsar.

Jub. The resolution fits a Roman senate. But, Cato, lend me for a while thy patience, And condescend to hear a young man speak. My father, when, some days before his death, He order'd me to march for Utica, (Alas! I thought not then his death so near!) Wept o'er me, press'd me in his aged arms, And, as his griefs gave way, "My son," said he, "Whatever fortune shall befal thy father, Be Cato's friend; he'll train thee up to great And virtuous deeds; do but observe him well, Thou'lt shun misfortunes, or thou'lt learn to bear them."

Cato. Juba, thy father was a worthy prince, And merited, alas! a better fate; But Heav'n thought otherwise.

Jub. My father's fate, In spite of all the fortitude that shines Before my face, in Cato's great example, Subdues my soul, and fills my eyes with tears.

Cato. It is an honest sorrow, and becomes thee.

Jub. My father drew respect from foreign climes: The kings of Afric sought him for their friend; Kings far remote, that rule, as fame reports, Behind the hidden sources of the Nile, In distant worlds, on t'other side the sun; Oft have their black ambassadors appear'd, Loaden with gifts, and fill'd the courts of Zama.

Cato. I am no stranger to thy father's greatness.

Jub. I would not boast the greatness of my father, But point out new alliances to Cato. Had we not better leave this Utica, To arm Numidia in our cause, and court Th' assistance of my father's powerful friends? Did they know Cato, our remotest kings Would pour embattled multitudes about him: Their swarthy hosts would darken all our plains, Doubling the native horror of the war, And making death more grim.

Cato. And canst thou think Cato will fly before the sword of Cæsar? Reduced, like Hannibal, to seek relief From court to court, and wander up and down A vagabond in Afric?

Jub. Cato, perhaps I'm too officious; but my forward cares Would fain preserve a life of so much value. My heart is wounded, when I see such virtue Afflicted by the weight of such misfortunes.

Cato. Thy nobleness of soul obliges me. But know, young prince, that valour soars above What the world calls misfortune and affliction. These are not ills; else would they never fall On Heav'n's first fav'rites, and the best of men. The gods, in bounty, work up storms about us, That give mankind occasion to exert Their hidden strength, and throw out into practice Virtues, which shun the day, and lie conceal'd In the smooth seasons and the calms of life.

Jub. I'm charm'd, whene'er thou talk'st; I pant for virtue, And all my soul endeavours at perfection.

Cato. Dost thou love watchings, abstinence, and toil, Laborious virtues all? Learn them from Cato; Success and fortune must thou learn from Cæsar.

Jub. The best good fortune that can fall on Juba, The whole success at which my heart aspires, Depends on Cato.

Cato. What does Juba say? Thy words confound me.

Jub. I would fain retract them. Give them me back again: they aimed at nothing.

Cato. Tell me thy wish, young prince; make not my ear A stranger to thy thoughts.

Jub. Oh! they're extravagant; Still let me hide them.

Cato. What can Juba ask, That Cato will refuse?

Jub. I fear to name it. Marcia–inherits all her father's virtues.

Cato. What wouldst thou say?

Jub. Cato, thou hast a daughter.

Cato. Adieu, young prince; I would not hear a word Should lessen thee in my esteem. Remember, The hand of fate is over us, and Heav'n Exacts severity from all our thoughts. It is not now a time to talk of aught But chains or conquest, liberty or death.

[*Exit*

Enter SYPHAX

Syph. How's this, my prince? What, cover'd with confusion? You look as if yon stern philosopher Had just now chid you.

Jub. Syphax, I'm undone!

Syph. I know it well.

Jub. Cato thinks meanly of me.

Syph. And so will all mankind.

Jub. I've open'd to him The weakness of my soul– my love for Marcia.

Syph. Cato's a proper person to intrust A love-tale with!

Jub. Oh, I could pierce my heart, My foolish heart!

Syph. Alas, my prince, how are you changed of late! I've known young Juba rise before the sun, To beat the thicket where the tiger slept, Or seek the lion in his dreadful haunts. I've seen you, Ev'n in the Lybian dog-days, hunt him down, Then charge him close, And, stooping from your horse, Rivet the panting savage to the ground.

Jub. Pr'ythee, no more.

Syph. How would the old king smile, To see you weigh the paws, when tipp'd with gold, And throw the shaggy spoils about your shoulders!

Jub. Syphax, this old man's talk, though honey flow'd In ev'ry word, would now lose all its sweetness. Cato's displeased, and Marcia lost forever.

Syph. Young prince, I yet could give you good advice; Marcia might still be yours.

Jub. As how, dear Syphax?

Syph. Juba commands Numidia's hardy troops, Mounted on steeds unused to the restraint Of curbs or bits, and fleeter than the winds: Give but the word, we snatch this damsel up, And bear her off.

Jub. Can such dishonest thoughts Rise up in man? Wouldst thou seduce my youth To do an act that would destroy mine honour?

Syph. Gods, I could tear my hair to hear you talk! Honour's a fine imaginary notion, That draws in raw and inexperienced men To real mischiefs, while they hunt a shadow.

Jub. Wouldst thou degrade thy prince into a ruffian?

Syph. The boasted ancestors of these great men, Whose virtues you admire, were all such ruffians. This dread of nations, this almighty Rome, That comprehends in her wide empire's bounds All under Heav'n, was founded on a rape; Your Scipios, Cæsars, Pompeys, and your Catos (The gods on earth), are all the spurious blood Of violated maids, of ravish'd Sabines.

Jub. Syphax, I fear that hoary head of thine Abounds too much in our Numidian wiles.

Syph. Indeed, my prince, you want to know the world.

Jub. If knowledge of the world makes men perfidious, May Juba ever live in ignorance!

Syph. Go, go; you're young.

Jub. Gods, must I tamely bear This arrogance, unanswer'd! Thou'rt a traitor, A false old traitor.

Syph. I've gone too far.   [*Aside*

Jub. Cato shall know the baseness of thy soul.

Syph. I must appease this storm, or perish in it.

[*Aside*

Young prince, behold these locks, that are grown white Beneath a helmet in your father's battles.

Jub. Those locks shall ne'er protect thy insolence.

Syph. Must one rash word, the infirmity of age, Throw down the merit of my better years? This the reward of a whole life of service!– Curse on the boy! how steadily he hears me!

[*Aside*

Jub. Syphax, no more! I would not hear you talk.

Syph. Not hear me talk! what, when my faith to Juba, My royal master's son, is call'd in question? My prince may strike me dead, and I'll be dumb; But whilst I live I must not hold my tongue, And languish out old age in his displeasure.

Jub. Thou know'st the way too well into my heart. I do believe thee loyal to thy prince.

Syph. What greater instance can I give? I've offer'd To do an action which my soul abhors, And gain you whom you love, at any price.

Jub. Was this thy motive? I have been too hasty.

Syph. And 'tis for this my prince has call'd me traitor.

Jub. Sure thou mistakest; I did not call thee so.

Syph. You did, indeed, my prince, you call'd me traitor. Nay, further, threatened you'd complain to Cato. Of what, my prince, would you complain to Cato? That Syphax loves you, and would sacrifice His life, nay, more, his honour, in your service?

Jub. Syphax, I know thou lovest me; but indeed Thy zeal for Juba carried thee too far. Honour's a sacred tie, the law of kings, The noble mind's distinguishing perfection, That aids and strengthens Virtue where it meets her, And imitates her actions where she is not; It ought not to be sported with.

Syph. Believe me, prince, you make old Syphax weep To hear you talk–but 'tis with tears of joy. If e'er your father's crown adorn your brows, Numidia will be blest by Cato's lectures.

Jub. Syphax, thy hand; we'll mutually forget The warmth of youth, and forwardness of age: Thy prince esteems thy worth, and loves thy person. If e'er the sceptre come into my hand, Syphax shall stand the second in my kingdom.

Syph. Why will you overwhelm my age with kindness? My joys grow burdensome, I sha'n't support it.

Jub. Syphax, farewell. I'll hence, and try to find Some blest occasion, that may set me right In Cato's thoughts. I'd rather have that man Approve my deeds, than worlds for my admirers.   [*Exit*

Syph. Young men soon give, and soon forget, affronts; Old age is slow in both–A false old traitor! These words, rash boy, may chance to cost thee dear. My heart had still some foolish fondness for thee; But hence, 'tis gone! I give it to the winds: Cæsar, I'm wholly thine.

Enter SEMPRONIUS.

All hail, Sempronius! Well, Cato's senate is resolved to wait The fury of a siege, before it yields.

Sem. Syphax, we both were on the verge of fate; Lucius declared for peace, and terms were offer'd To Cato, by a messenger from Cæsar. Should they submit, ere our designs are ripe, We both must perish in the common wreck, Lost in the general, undistinguish'd ruin.

Syph. But how stands Cato?

Sem. Thou hast seen mount Atlas: Whilst storms and tempests thunder on its brows, And oceans break their billows at its feet, It stands unmoved, and glories in its height; Such is that haughty man; his tow'ring soul, 'Midst all the shocks and injuries of fortune, Rises superior, and looks down on Cæsar.

Syph. But what's this messenger?

Sem. I've practised with him, And found a means to let the victor know That Syphax and Sempronius are

his friends. But let me now examine in my turn; Is
Juba fix'd?

Syph. Yes—but it is to Cato. I've tried the force of
every reason on him, Soothed and caress'd; been
angry, soothed again; Laid safety, life, and interest in
his sight; But all are vain, he scorns them all for
Cato.

Sem. Come, 'tis no matter; we shall do without him.
He'll make a pretty figure in a triumph, And serve to
trip before the victor's chariot. Syphax, I now may
hope thou hast forsook Thy Juba's cause, and
wishest Marcia mine.

Syph. May she be thine as fast as thou wouldst have
her.

Sem. Syphax, I love that woman; though I curse Her
and myself, yet, spite of me, I love her.

Syph. Make Cato sure, and give up Utica, Cæsar will
ne'er refuse thee such a trifle. But are thy troops
prepared for a revolt? Does the sedition catch from
man to man, And run among the ranks?

Sem. All, all is ready; The factious leaders are our
friends, that spread Murmurs and discontents
among the soldiers; They count their toilsome
marches, long fatigues, Unusual fastings, and will
hear no more This medley of philosophy and war.
Within an hour they'll storm the senate house.

Syph. Meanwhile I'll draw up my Numidian troops Within the square, to exercise their arms, And, as I see occasion, favour thee. I laugh, to see how your unshaken Cato Will look aghast, while unforeseen destruction Pours in upon him thus from every side. So, where our wide Numidian wastes extend, Sudden th' impetuous hurricanes descend, Wheel through the air, in circling eddies play, Tear up the sands, and sweep whole plains away. The helpless traveller, with wild surprise, Sees the dry desert all around him rise, And, smother'd in the dusty whirlwind, dies. [*Exeunt*

Act *the* Third

Scene I

A Chamber

Enter MARCUS *and* PORTIUS

Marc. Thanks to my stars, I have not ranged about The wilds of life, ere I could find a friend; Nature first pointed out my Portius to me, And early taught me, by her secret force, To love thy person, ere I knew thy merit, Till what was instinct, grew up into friendship.

Por. Marcus, the friendships of the world are oft Confed'racies in vice, or leagues of pleasure; Ours has severest virtue for its basis, And such a friendship ends not but with life.

Marc. Portius, thou know'st my soul in all its weakness; Then, pr'ythee, spare me on its tender side; Indulge me but in love, my other passions Shall rise and fall by virtue's nicest rules.

Por. When love's well-timed, 'tis not a fault to love. The strong, the brave, the virtuous, and the wise, Sink in the soft captivity together.

Marc. Alas, thou talk'st like one that never felt Th' impatient throbs and longings of a soul, That pants and reaches after distant good! A lover does not live by vulgar time; Believe me, Portius, in my Lucia's absence Life hangs upon me, and becomes a burden; And yet, when I behold the charming maid, I'm ten times more undone; while hope and fear, And grief and rage, and love, rise up at once, And with variety of pain distract me.

Por. What can thy Portius do to give thee help?

Marc. Portius, thou oft enjoy'st the fair one's presence; Then undertake my cause, and plead it to her With all the strength and heat of eloquence Fraternal love and friendship can inspire. Tell her thy brother languishes to death, And fades away, and withers in his bloom; That he forgets his sleep, and loathes his food; That youth, and health, and war, are joyless to him; Describe his anxious days, and restless nights, And all the torments that thou see'st me suffer.

Por. Marcus, I beg thee give me not an office, That suits with me so ill. Thou know'st my temper.

Marc. Wilt thou behold me sinking in my woes, And wilt thou not reach out a friendly arm, To raise me from amidst this plunge of sorrows?

Por. Marcus, thou canst not ask what I'd refuse; But here, believe me, I've a thousand reasons—

Marc. I know thou'lt say my passion's out of season, That Cato's great example and misfortunes Should both conspire to drive it from my thoughts. But what's all this to one that loves like me? O Portius, Portius, from my soul I wish Thou did'st but know thyself what 'tis to love! Then wouldst thou pity and assist thy brother.

Por. What should I do? If I disclose my passion, Our friendship's at an end: if I conceal it, The world will call me false to a friend and brother.   [*Aside*

Marc. But see, where Lucia, at her wonted hour, Amid the cool of yon high marble arch, Enjoys the noon-day breeze! Observe her, Portius; That face, that shape, those eyes, that heav'n of beauty! Observe her well, and blame me if thou canst.

Por. She sees us, and advances—

Marc. I'll withdraw, And leave you for a while. Remember, Portius, Thy brother's life depends upon thy tongue.   [*Exit*

Enter LUCIA.

Lucia. Did not I see your brother Marcus here? Why did he fly the place, and shun my presence?

Por. Oh, Lucia, language is too faint to show His rage of love; it preys upon his life; He pines, he sickens, he despairs, he dies!

Lucia. How wilt thou guard thy honour, in the shock Of love and friendship! Think betimes, my Portius, Think how the nuptial tie, that might ensure Our mutual bliss, would raise to such a height Thy brother's griefs, as might perhaps destroy him.

Por. Alas, poor youth! What dost thou think, my Lucia? His gen'rous, open, undesigning heart Has begg'd his rival to solicit for him! Then do not strike him dead with a denial.

Lucia. No, Portius, no; I see thy sister's tears, Thy father's anguish, and thy brother's death, In the pursuit of our ill-fated loves; And, Portius, here I swear, to Heav'n I swear, To Heav'n, and all the powers that judge mankind, Never to mix my plighted hands with thine, While such a cloud of mischief hangs upon us, But to forget our loves, and drive thee out From all my thoughts—as far as I am able.

Por. What hast thou said? I'm thunderstruck—recall Those hasty words, or I am lost forever.

Lucia. Has not the vow already pass'd my lips? The gods have heard it, and 'tis seal'd in heav'n. May all the vengeance that was ever pour'd On perjured heads, o'erwhelm me if I break it!

Por. Fix'd in astonishment, I gaze upon thee, Like one just blasted by a stroke from heav'n, Who pants for breath and stiffens, yet alive, In dreadful looks, a monument of wrath!

Lucia. Think, Portius, think thou see'st thy dying brother Stabb'd at his heart, and all besmear'd with blood, Storming at Heav'n and thee! Thy awful sire Sternly demands the cause, the accursed cause, That robs him of his son: poor Marcia trembles, Then tears her hair, and, frantic in her griefs, Calls out on Lucia. What could Lucia answer, Or how stand up in such a scene of sorrow?

Por. To my confusion and eternal grief, I must approve the sentence that destroys me.

Lucia. Portius, no more; thy words shoot through my heart, Melt my resolves, and turn me all to love. Why are those tears of fondness in thy eyes? Why heaves thy heart? Why swells thy soul with sorrow? It softens me too much—Farewell, my Portius! Farewell, though death is in the word,—forever!

Por. Stay, Lucia, stay! What dost thou say? Forever? Thou must not go; my soul still hovers o'er thee, And can't get loose.

Lucia. If the firm Portius shake, To hear of parting, think what Lucia suffers!

Por. 'Tis true, unruffled and serene, I've met The common accidents of life, but here Such an unlook'd-for storm of ills falls on me. It beats down all my strength—I cannot bear it. We must not part.

Lucia. What dost thou say? Not part! Hast thou forgot the vow that I have made? Are not there heavens, and gods, that thunder o'er us? —But see, thy brother Marcus bends this way; I sicken at the sight. Once more, farewell. Farewell, and know, thou wrong'st me, if thou think'st Ever was love or ever grief like mine. [*Exit* LUCIA

Enter MARCUS.

Marc. Portius, what hopes? How stands she? am I doom'd To life or death?

Por. What wouldst thou have me say?

Marc. What means this pensive posture? Thou appear'st Like one amazed and terrified.

Por. I've reason.

Marc. Thy downcast looks, and thy disorder'd thoughts, Tell me my fate. I ask not the success My cause has found.

Por. I'm grieved I undertook it.

Marc. What, does the barbarous maid insult my heart, My aching heart, and triumph in my pains? That I could cast her from my thoughts forever!

Por. Away! you're too suspicious in your griefs; Lucia, though sworn never to think of love, Compassionates your pains, and pities you.

Marc. Compassionates my pains, and pities me! What is compassion, when 'tis void of love? Fool that I was, to choose so cold a friend To urge my cause!—Compassionates my pains! Pr'ythee what art, what rhet'ric didst thou use To gain this mighty boon?—She pities me! To one that asks the warm returns of love, Compassion's cruelty, 'tis scorn, 'tis death—

Por. Marcus, no more; have I deserved this treatment?

Marc. What have I said? Oh! Portius, Oh, forgive me! A soul exasperated in ills, falls out With everything—its friend, itself—but hah!   [*Shout* What means that shout, big with the sounds of war? What new alarm?

Por. A second, louder yet, Swells in the wind, and comes more full upon us.

Marc. Oh, for some glorious cause to fall in battle! Lucia, thou hast undone me: thy disdain Has broke my heart; 'tis death must give me ease.

Por. Quick let us hence. Who knows if Cato's life Stands sure? Oh, Marcus, I am warm'd; my heart Leaps at the trumpet's voice, and burns for glory.
                                          [*Exeunt*

Scene II

Part of the Senate House

Enter SEMPRONIUS, *with* LEADERS *of the Mutiny.*

Sem. At length the winds are raised, the storm blows high! Be it your care, my friends, to keep it up In all its fury, and direct it right, Till it has spent itself on Cato's head. Meanwhile, I'll herd among his friends, and seem One of the number, that, whate'er arrive, My friends and fellow soldiers may be safe.

[*Exit*

1 Lead. We are all safe; Sempronius is our friend. Sempronius is as brave a man as Cato. But, hark, he enters. Bear up boldly to him; Be sure you beat him down, and bind him fast; This day will end our toils. Fear nothing, for Sempronius is our friend.

Enter SEMPRONIUS, *with* CATO, LUCIUS, PORTIUS, *and* MARCUS

Cato. Where are those bold, intrepid sons of war, That greatly turn their backs upon the foe, And to their general send a brave defiance?

Sem. Curse on their dastard souls, they stand astonish'd!

[*Aside*

Cato. Perfidious men! And will you thus dishonour Your past exploits, and sully all your wars? Why could not Cato fall Without your guilt! Behold, ungrateful men, Behold my bosom naked to your swords, And let the man that's injured strike the blow. Which of you all suspects that he is wrong'd, Or thinks he suffers greater ills than Cato? Am I distinguished from you but by toils, Superior toils, and heavier weight of cares? Painful pre-eminence!

Sem. Confusion to the villains! all is lost!

[*Aside*

Cato. Have you forgotten Lybia's burning waste, Its barren rocks, parch'd earth, and hills of sand, Its tainted air, and all its broods of poison? Who was the first to explore th' untrodden path, When life was hazarded in ev'ry step? Or, fainting in the long laborious march, When, on the banks of an unlook'd-for stream, You sunk the river with repeated draughts, Who was the last of all your host who thirsted?

Sem. Did not his temples glow In the same sultry winds and scorching heats?

Cato. Hence, worthless men! hence! and complain to Cæsar, You could not undergo the toil of war, Nor bear the hardships that your leader bore.

Lucius. See, Cato, see the unhappy men: they weep! Fear, and remorse, and sorrow for their crime, Appear in ev'ry look, and plead for mercy.

Cato. Learn to be honest men; give up yon leaders, And pardon shall descend on all the rest.

Sem. Cato, commit these wretches to my care; First let them each be broken on the rack, Then, with what life remains, impaled, and left To writhe at leisure round the bloody stake; There let them hang, and taint the southern wind. The partners of their crime will learn obedience.

Cato. Forbear, Sempronius!–see they suffer death, But in their deaths remember they are men; Strain not the laws, to make their tortures grievous. Lucius, the base, degen'rate age requires Severity. When by just vengeance guilty mortals perish, The gods behold the punishment with pleasure, And lay th' uplifted thunderbolt aside.

Sem. Cato, I execute thy will with pleasure.

Cato. Meanwhile, we'll sacrifice to liberty. Remember, O my friends! the laws, the rights, The gen'rous plan of power delivered down From age to age by your renown'd forefathers, (So dearly bought, the price of so much blood:) Oh, let it never perish in your hands! But piously transmit it to your children. Do thou, great liberty, inspire our souls, And make our lives in thy possession happy, Or our deaths glorious in thy just defence.

[*Exeunt* CATO, *etc.*

1 Lead. Sempronius, you have acted like yourself. One would have thought you had been half in earnest.

Sem. Villain, stand off; base, grov'ling, worthless wretches, Mongrels in faction, poor faint-hearted traitors!

1 Lead. Nay, now, you carry it too far, Sempronius!

Sem. Know, villains, when such paltry slaves presume To mix in treason, if the plot succeeds, They're thrown neglected by; but if it fails, They're sure to die like dogs, as you shall do. Here, take these factious monsters, drag them forth To sudden death.

1 Lead. Nay, since it comes to this—

Sem. Dispatch them quick, but first pluck out their tongues, Lest with their dying breath they sow sedition.

[*Exeunt* GUARDS, *with their* LEADERS

Enter SYPHAX.

Syph. Our first design, my friend, has proved abortive; Still there remains an after-game to play; My troops are mounted; Let but Sempronius head us in our flight, We'll force the gate where Marcus keeps his guard, And hew down all that would oppose our passage. A day will bring us into Cæsar's camp.

Sem. Confusion! I have fail'd of half my purpose: Marcia, the charming Marcia's left behind!

Syph. How! will Sempronius turn a woman's slave?

Sem. Think not thy friend can ever feel the soft Unmanly warmth and tenderness of love. Syphax, I long to clasp that haughty maid, And bend her stubborn virtue to my passion: When I have gone thus far, I'd cast her off.

Syph. Well said! that's spoken like thyself, Sempronius! What hinders, then, but that thou find her out, And hurry her away by manly force?

Sem. But how to gain admission? For access Is given to none but Juba, and her brothers.

Syph. Thou shalt have Juba's dress, and Juba's guards; The doors will open, when Numidia's prince Seems to appear before the slaves that watch them.

Sem. Heavens, what a thought is there! Marcia's my own! How will my bosom swell with anxious joy, When I behold her struggling in my arms, With glowing beauty, and disorder'd charms, While fear and anger, with alternate grace, Pant in her breast, and vary in her face! So Pluto seized off Proserpine, convey'd To hell's tremendous gloom th' affrighted maid; There grimly smiled, pleased with the beauteous prize, Nor envied Jove his sunshine and his skies.   [Exeunt

Act *the* Fourth

Scene I

A Chamber

Enter LUCIA *and* MARCIA

Lucia. Now, tell me, Marcia, tell me from thy soul, If thou believest 'tis possible for woman To suffer greater ills than Lucia suffers?

Marcia Oh, Lucia, Lucia, might my big swol'n heart Vent all its griefs, and give a loose to sorrow, Marcia could answer thee in sighs, keep pace With all thy woes, and count out tear for tear.

Lucia. I know thou'rt doom'd alike to be beloved By Juba, and thy father's friend, Sempronius: But which of these has power to charm like Portius?

Marcia. Still, I must beg thee not to name Sempronius. Lucia, I like not that loud, boist'rous man. Juba, to all the bravery of a hero, Adds softest love, and more than female sweetness; Juba might make the proudest of our sex, Any of womankind, but Marcia, happy.

Lucia. And why not Marcia? Come, you strive in vain To hide your thoughts from one who knows too well The inward glowings of a heart in love.

Marcia. While Cato lives, his daughter has no right To love or hate, but as his choice directs.

Lucia. But should this father give you to Sempronius?

Marcia. I dare not think he will: but if he should– Why wilt thou add to all the griefs I suffer, Imaginary ills, and fancied tortures? I hear the sound of feet! They march this way. Let us retire, and try if we can drown Each softer thought in sense of present danger: When love once pleads admission to our hearts, In spite of all the virtues we can boast, The woman that deliberates is lost.   [*Exeunt*

Enter SEMPRONIUS, *dressed like* JUBA,
with NUMIDIAN GUARDS.

Sem. The deer is lodged, I've track'd her to her covert. How will the young Numidian rave to see His mistress lost! If aught could glad my soul, Beyond the enjoyment of so bright a prize, 'Twould be to torture that young, gay barbarian. –But, hark! what noise! Death to my hopes! 'tis he, 'Tis Juba's self! there is but one way left—

Enter JUBA.

Jub. What do I see? Who's this that dares usurp The guards and habits of Numidia's prince?

Sem. One that was born to scourge thy arrogance, Presumptuous youth!

Jub. What can this mean? Sempronius!

Sem. My sword shall answer thee. Have at thy heart.

Jub. Nay then, beware thy own, proud, barbarous man.

[SEMPRONIUS *falls*

Sem. Curse on my stars! Am I then doom'd to fall By a boy's hand, disfigured in a vile Numidian dress, and for a worthless woman? Gods, I'm distracted! this my close of life! Oh, for a peal of thunder, that would make Earth, sea, and air, and heav'n, and Cato tremble! [*Dies*

Jub. I'll hence to Cato, That we may there at length unravel all This dark design, this mystery of fate.

[*Exit* JUBA

Enter LUCIA *and* MARCIA.

Lucia. Sure 'twas the clash of swords; my troubled heart Is so cast down, and sunk amidst its sorrows, It throbs with fear, and aches at ev'ry sound. Oh, Marcia, should thy brothers, for my sake— I die away with horror at the thought!

Marcia. See, Lucia, see! here's blood! here's blood and murder! Ha! a Numidian! Heav'n preserve the prince! The face lies muffled up within the garment, But ah! death to my sight! a diadem, And royal robes! O gods! 'tis he, 'tis he! Juba lies dead before us!

Lucia. Now, Marcia, now, call up to thy assistance Thy wonted strength and constancy of mind; Thou canst not put it to a greater trial.

Marcia. Lucia, look there, and wonder at my patience; Have I not cause to rave, and beat my breast, To rend my heart with grief, and run distracted?

Lucia. What can I think, or say, to give thee comfort?

Marcia. Talk not of comfort, 'tis for lighter ills: Behold a sight that strikes all comfort dead.

Enter JUBA, *listening.*

I will indulge my sorrows, and give way To all the pangs and fury of despair; That man, that best of men, deserved it from me.

Jub. What do I hear? and was the false Sempronius That best of men? Oh, had I fall'n like him, And could have been thus mourn'd, I had been happy.

Marcia. 'Tis not in fate to ease my tortured breast. Oh, he was all made up of love and charms! Whatever maid could wish, or man admire: Delight of every eye; when he appear'd, A secret pleasure gladden'd all that saw him; But when he talk'd, the proudest Roman blush'd To hear his virtues, and old age grew wise. Oh, Juba! Juba!

Jub. What means that voice? Did she not call on Juba?

Marcia. Why do I think on what he was? he's dead! He's dead, and never knew how much I loved him! Lucia, who knows but his poor, bleeding heart, Amidst its agonies, remember'd Marcia, And the last words he utter'd call'd me cruel! Alas! he knew not, hapless youth, he knew not Marcia's whole soul was full of love and Juba!

Jub. Where am I? Do I live? or am indeed What Marcia thinks? All is Elysium round me!

Marcia. Ye dear remains of the most loved of men, Nor modesty nor virtue here forbid A last embrace, while thus—

Jub. See, Marcia, see,   [*Throwing himself before her* The happy Juba lives! he lives to catch That dear embrace, and to return it too, With mutual warmth, and eagerness of love.

Marcia. With pleasure and amaze I stand transported! If thou art Juba, who lies there?

Jub. A wretch, Disguised like Juba on a cursed design. I could not bear To leave thee in the neighbourhood of death, But flew, in all the haste of love, to find thee; I found thee weeping, and confess this once, Am rapt with joy, to see my Marcia's tears.

Marcia. I've been surprised in an unguarded hour, But must not go back; the love, that lay Half smother'd in my breast, has broke through all Its weak restraints, and burns in its full lustre. I cannot, if I would, conceal it from thee.

Jub. My joy, my best beloved, my only wish! How shall I speak the transport of my soul!

Marcia. Lucia, thy arm. Lead to my apartment. Oh! prince! I blush to think what I have said, But fate has wrested the confession from me; Go on, and prosper in the paths of honour. Thy virtue will excuse my passion for thee, And make the gods propitious to our love.

[*Exeunt* MARCIA *and* LUCIA

Jub. I am so blest, I fear 'tis all a dream. Fortune, thou now hast made amends for all Thy past unkindness: I absolve my stars. What though Numidia add her conquer'd towns And provinces to swell the victor's triumph, Juba will never at his fate repine: Let Cæsar have the world, if Marcia's mine.

[*Exit*

Scene II

The Street

A March at a distance

Enter CATO *and* LUCIUS

Luc. I stand astonish'd! What, the bold Sempronius, That still broke foremost through the crowd of patriots, As with a hurricane of zeal transported, And virtuous even to madness–

Cato. Trust me, Lucius, Our civil discords have produced such crimes, Such monstrous crimes, I am surprized at nothing. –Oh Lucius, I am sick of this bad world! The daylight and the sun grow painful to me.

Enter PORTIUS.

But see, where Portius comes: what means this haste? Why are thy looks thus changed?

Por. My heart is grieved, I bring such news as will afflict my father.

Cato. Has Cæsar shed more Roman blood?

Por. Not so. The traitor Syphax, as within the square He exercised his troops, the signal given, Flew off at once with his Numidian horse To the south gate, where Marcus holds the watch; I saw, and call'd to stop him, but in vain: He toss'd his arm aloft, and proudly told me, He would not stay, and perish, like Sempronius.

Cato. Perfidious man! But haste, my son, and see Thy brother Marcus acts a Roman's part.

                         [*Exit* PORTIUS

–Lucius, the torrent bears too hard upon me: Justice gives way to force: the conquer'd world Is Cæsar's! Cato has no business in it.

Luc. While pride, oppression, and injustice reign, The world will still demand her Cato's presence. In pity to mankind submit to Cæsar, And reconcile thy mighty soul to life.

Cato. Would Lucius have me live to swell the number Of Cæsar's slaves, or by a base submission Give up the cause of Rome, and own a tyrant?

Luc. The victor never will impose on Cato Ungen'rous terms. His enemies confess The virtues of humanity are Cæsar's.

Cato. Curse on his virtues! they've undone his country. Such popular humanity is treason— But see young Juba; the good youth appears, Full of the guilt of his perfidious subjects!

Luc. Alas, poor prince! his fate deserves compassion.

Enter JUBA.

Jub. I blush, and am confounded to appear Before thy presence, Cato.

Cato. What's thy crime?

Jub. I'm a Numidian.

Cato. And a brave one, too. Thou hast a Roman soul.

Jub. Hast thou not heard of my false countrymen?

Cato. Alas, young prince! Falsehood and fraud shoot up in ev'ry soil, The product of all climes—Rome has its Cæsars.

Jub. 'Tis generous thus to comfort the distress'd.

Cato. 'Tis just to give applause, where 'tis deserved: Thy virtue, prince, has stood the test of fortune, Like purest gold, that, tortured in the furnace, Comes out more bright, and brings forth all its weight.

Jub. What shall I answer thee? I'd rather gain Thy praise, O Cato! than Numidia's empire.

Enter PORTIUS.

Por. Misfortune on misfortune! grief on grief! My brother Marcus—

Cato. Ha! what has he done? Has he forsook his post? Has he given way? Did he look tamely on, and let them pass?

Por. Scarce had I left my father, but I met him Borne on the shields of his surviving soldiers, Breathless and pale, and cover'd o'er with wounds. Long, at the head of his few faithful friends, He stood the shock of a whole host of foes, Till, obstinately brave, and bent on death, Oppress'd with multitudes, he greatly fell.

Cato. I'm satisfied.

Por. Nor did he fall, before His sword had pierced thro' the false heart of Syphax. Yonder he lies. I saw the hoary traitor Grin in the pangs of death, and bite the ground.

Cato. Thanks to the gods, my boy has done his duty. –Portius, when I am dead, be sure you place His urn near mine.

Por. Long may they keep asunder!

Luc. Oh, Cato, arm thy soul with all its patience; See where the corpse of thy dead son approaches! The citizens and senators alarm'd, Have gather'd round it, and attend it weeping.

CATO *meeting the Corpse.*–SENATORS *attending.*

Cato. Welcome, my son! Here lay him down, my friends, Full in my sight, that I may view at leisure The bloody corse, and count those glorious wounds. –How beautiful is death, when earn'd by virtue! Who would not be that youth? What pity is it, That we can die but once, to serve our country! –Why sits this sadness on your brows, my friends? I should have blush'd, if Cato's house had stood Secure, and flourish'd in a civil war. Portius, behold thy brother, and remember, Thy life is not thy own when Rome demands it.

Jub. Was ever man like this!

Cato. Alas, my friends, Why mourn you thus? let not a private loss Afflict your hearts. 'Tis Rome requires our tears, The mistress of the world, the seat of empire, The nurse of heroes, the delight of gods, That humbled the proud tyrants of the earth, And set the nations free; Rome is no more. Oh, liberty! Oh, virtue! Oh, my country!

Jub. Behold that upright man! Rome fills his eyes With tears, that flow'd not o'er his own dear son.

[*Aside*

Cato. Whate'er the Roman virtue has subdued, The sun's whole course, the day and year, are Cæsar's: For him the self-devoted Decii died, The Fabii fell, and the great Scipios conquer'd: Ev'n Pompey fought for Cæsar. Oh, my friends, How is the toil of fate, the work of ages, The Roman empire, fall'n! Oh, cursed ambition! Fall'n into Cæsar's hands! Our great forefathers Had left him nought to conquer but his country.

Jub. While Cato lives, Cæsar will blush to see Mankind enslaved, and be ashamed of empire.

Cato. Cæsar ashamed! Has he not seen Pharsalia?

Luc. 'Tis time thou save thyself and us.

Cato. Lose not a thought on me; I'm out of danger: Heaven will not leave me in the victor's hand. Cæsar shall never say, he conquer'd Cato. But oh, my friends! your safety fills my heart With anxious thoughts; a thousand secret terrors Rise in my soul. How shall I save my friends? 'Tis now, O Cæsar, I begin to fear thee!

Luc. Cæsar has mercy, if we ask it of him.

Cato. Then ask it, I conjure you; let him know, Whate'er was done against him, Cato did it. Add, if you please, that I request of him,– That I myself, with tears, request it of him,– The virtue of my friends may pass unpunish'd. Juba, my heart is troubled for thy sake. Should I advise thee to regain Numidia, Or seek the conqueror?

Jub. If I forsake thee Whilst I have life, may Heaven abandon Juba!

Cato. Thy virtues, prince, if I foresee aright, Will one day make thee great; at Rome, hereafter, 'Twill be no crime to have been Cato's friend. Portius, draw near: my son, thou oft hast seen Thy sire engaged in a corrupted state, Wrestling with vice and faction: now thou see'st me Spent, overpower'd, despairing of success. Let me advise thee to retreat betimes To thy paternal seat, the Sabine field; Where the great Censor toil'd with his own hands, And all our frugal ancestors were bless'd In humble virtues, and a rural life; There live retired, pray for the peace of Rome; Content thyself to be obscurely good. When vice prevails, and impious men bear sway, The post of honour is a private station.

Por. I hope my father does not recommend A life to Portius that he scorns himself.

Cato. Farewell, my friends! If there be any of you Who dare not trust the victor's clemency, Know there are ships prepared, by my command, That shall convey you to the wish'd-for port. Is there aught else, my friends, I can do for you? The conqueror draws near. Once more, farewell! If e'er we meet hereafter, we shall meet In happier climes, and on a safer shore, Where Cæsar never shall approach us more.   [*Pointing to his dead son* There, the brave youth, with love of virtue fired, Who greatly in his country's cause expired, Shall know he conquer'd. The firm patriot there, Who made the welfare of mankind his care, Though still by faction, vice, and fortune crost, Shall find the gen'rous labour was not lost.   [*Exeunt*

Act *the* Fifth

Scene I

A Chamber

CATO *solus, sitting in a thoughtful Posture; in his Hand, Plato's Book on the Immortality of the Soul. A drawn Sword on the Table by him.*

Cato. It must be so–Plato, thou reason'st well– Else whence this pleasing hope, this fond desire, This longing after immortality? Or whence this secret dread, and inward horror, Of falling into nought? Why shrinks the soul Back on herself, and startles at destruction? 'Tis the divinity that stirs within us; 'Tis Heav'n itself that points out an hereafter, And intimates eternity to man. Eternity! thou pleasing, dreadful thought! Through what variety of untried being, Through what new scenes and changes must we pass? The wide, the unbounded prospect lies before me; But shadows, clouds, and darkness, rest upon it. Here will I hold. If there's a Power above us (And that there is, all Nature cries aloud Through all her works), He must delight in virtue; And that which He delights in must be happy. But when, or where?–this world was made for Cæsar: I'm weary of conjectures–this must end them.

　　　　　　　　　　　　　　[*Laying his hand upon his sword*

Thus am I doubly arm'd: my death and life, My bane and antidote, are both before me. This in a moment brings me to an end; But this informs me I shall never die. The soul, secured in her existence, smiles At the drawn dagger, and defies its point. The stars shall fade away, the sun himself Grow dim with age, and nature sink in years, But thou shalt flourish in immortal youth, Unhurt amidst the war of elements, The wreck of matter, and the crush of worlds. What means this heaviness, that hangs upon me? This lethargy, that creeps through all my senses? Nature, oppress'd and harass'd out with care, Sinks down to rest. This once I'll favour her, That my awaken'd soul may take her flight, Renew'd in all her strength, and fresh with life, An offering lit for Heav'n. Let guilt or fear Disturb man's rest, Cato knows neither of them, Indiff'rent in his choice to sleep or die.

Enter PORTIUS.

But, hah! who's this? my son! Why this intrusion? Were not my orders that I would be private? Why am I disobey'd?

Por. Alas, my father! What means this sword, this instrument of death? Let me convey it hence.

Cato. Rash youth, forbear!

Por. Oh, let the pray'rs, th' entreaties of your friends, Their tears, their common danger, wrest it from you!

Cato. Wouldst thou betray me? Wouldst thou give me up, A slave, a captive, into Cæsar's hands? Retire, and learn obedience to a father, Or know, young man—

Por. Look not thus sternly on me; You know, I'd rather die than disobey you.

Cato. 'Tis well! again I'm master of myself. Now, Cæsar, let thy troops beset our gates, And bar each avenue; thy gath'ring fleets O'erspread the sea, and stop up ev'ry port; Cato shall open to himself a passage, And mock thy hopes.——

Por. Oh, sir! forgive your son, Whose grief hangs heavy on him. Oh, my father! How am I sure it is not the last time I e'er shall call you so? Be not displeased, Oh, be not angry with me whilst I weep, And, in the anguish of my heart, beseech you To quit the dreadful purpose of your soul!

Cato. Thou hast been ever good and dutiful.
                              [*Embracing him.*
Weep not, my son, all will be well again; The righteous gods, whom I have sought to please, Will succour Cato, and preserve his children.

Por. Your words give comfort to my drooping heart.

Cato. Portius, thou may'st rely upon my conduct: Thy father will not act what misbecomes him. But go, my son, and see if aught be wanting Among thy father's friends; see them embark'd, And tell me if the winds and seas befriend them. My soul is quite weigh'd down with care, and asks The soft refreshment of a moment's sleep.

Por. My thoughts are more at ease, my heart revives

[*Exit* CATO

Enter MARCIA.

Oh, Marcia! Oh, my sister, still there's hope Our father will not cast away a life So needful to us all, and to his country. He is retired to rest, and seems to cherish Thoughts full of peace.—He has dispatch'd me hence With orders that bespeak a mind composed, And studious for the safety of his friends. Marcia, take care, that none disturb his slumbers.

[*Exit*

Marcia. Oh, ye immortal powers, that guard the just, Watch round his couch, and soften his repose, Banish his sorrows, and becalm his soul With easy dreams; remember all his virtues, And show mankind that goodness is your care!

Enter LUCIA.

Lucia. Where is your father, Marcia; where is Cato?

Marcia. Lucia, speak low, he is retired to rest. Lucia, I feel a gentle dawning hope Rise in my soul—We shall be happy still.

Lucia. Alas, I tremble when I think on Cato! In every view, in every thought, I tremble! Cato is stern and awful as a god; He knows not how to wink at human frailty, Or pardon weakness, that he never felt.

Marcia. Though stern and awful to the foes of Rome, He is all goodness, Lucia, always mild; Compassionate and gentle to his friends; Fill'd with domestic tenderness, the best, The kindest father; I have ever found him Easy and good, and bounteous to my wishes.

Lucia. 'Tis his consent alone can make us blest. Marcia, we both are equally involved In the same intricate, perplex'd distress. The cruel hand of fate, that has destroy'd Thy brother Marcus, whom we both lament—

Marcia. And ever shall lament; unhappy youth!

Lucia. Has set my soul at large, and now I stand Loose of my vow. But who knows Cato's thoughts? Who knows how yet he may dispose of Portius, Or how he has determined of himself?

Marcia. Let him but live, commit the rest to Heav'n.

Enter LUCIUS.

Luc. Sweet are the slumbers of the virtuous man! Oh, Marcia, I have seen thy godlike father! Some power invisible supports his soul, And bears it up in

all its wonted greatness. A kind, refreshing sleep is
fall'n upon him: I saw him stretch'd at ease; his
fancy lost In pleasing dreams; as I drew near his
couch, He smiled, and cried, "Cæsar, thou canst not
hurt me."

Marcia. His mind still labours with some dreadful
thought.

Enter JUBA.

Jub. Lucius, the horsemen are return'd from viewing
The number, strength, and posture of our foes,
Who now encamp within a short hour's march; On
the high point of yon bright western tower, We ken
them from afar; the setting sun Plays on their
shining arms and burnish'd helmets, And covers all
the field with gleams of fire.

Luc. Marcia, 'tis time we should awake thy father.
Cæsar is still disposed to give us terms, And waits at
distance, till he hears from Cato.

Enter PORTIUS.

Portius, thy looks speak somewhat of importance,
What tidings dost thou bring? Methinks, I see
Unusual gladness sparkle in thy eyes.

Por. As I was hasting to the port, where now My
father's friends, impatient for a passage, Accuse the
ling'ring winds, a sail arrived From Pompey's son,
who, through the realms of Spain, Calls out for

vengeance on his father's death, And rouses the whole nation up to arms. Were Cato at their head, once more might Rome Assert her rights, and claim her liberty. But, hark! what means that groan?—Oh, give me way, And let me fly into my father's presence!   [*Exit*

Luc. Cato, amidst his slumbers, thinks on Rome, And, in the wild disorder of his soul, Mourns o'er his country.–Ha! a second groan– Heav'n guard us all!

Marcia. Alas, 'tis not the voice Of one who sleeps; 'tis agonizing pain– 'Tis death is in that sound—

Enter PORTIUS.

Por. Oh, sight of woe! Oh, Marcia, what we fear'd is come to pass– Cato has fall'n upon his sword—

Luc. Oh, Portius, Hide all the horrors of thy mournful tale, And let me guess the rest.

Por. I've raised him up, And placed him in his chair; where pale and faint, He gasps for breath, and, as his life flows from him, Demands to see his friends. His servants weeping, Obsequious to his order, bear him hither!—

Marcia. Oh, Heav'n! assist me in this dreadful hour, To pay the last sad duties to my father!

CATO *brought on, in a Chair.*

Cato. Here set me down— Portius, come near me– Are my friends embark'd? Can anything be thought of for their service? Whilst I yet live, let me not live in vain— Oh, Lucius, art thou here?–Thou art too good– Let this our friendship live between our children; Make Portius happy in thy daughter Lucia– – Marcia, my daughter— Oh, bend me forward!— Juba loves thee, Marcia– A senator of Rome, while Rome survived, Would not have match'd his daughter with a king– But Cæsar's arms have thrown down all distinction– I'm sick to death— Oh, when shall I get loose From this vain world, th' abode of guilt and sorrow! And yet, methinks, a beam of light breaks in On my departing soul— Alas, I fear I've been too hasty!–Oh, ye powers, that search The heart of man, and weigh his inmost thoughts, If I have done amiss, impute it not— The best may err, but you are good, and–Oh!– [*Dies*

Por. There fled the greatest soul that ever warm'd A Roman breast:– From hence, let fierce contending nations know, What dire effects from civil discord flow: 'Tis this that shakes our country with alarms; And gives up Rome a prey to Roman arms; Produces fraud, and cruelty, and strife, And robs the guilty world of Cato's life.   [*Exeunt omnes*

The End

CPSIA information can be obtained
at www.ICGtesting.com
Printed in the USA
LVHW101621230722
724098LV00003B/78